"RV Repair And Maintenance"

Congratulations: Here's your own easy to use RV Repair And Maintenance Log Book. The perfect way to track maintenance and repairs.

There's plenty of space for your notes as well for anything that needs future attention.

This **RV Maintenance and Repairs Log Book** allows you to keep safe accurate records where ever you are. Keep it in the glove box for easy access. Happy and safe travels :-)

RV Maintenance and Repairs Log Book. If found please contact

Name:..
Contact Number: ....
Email:..

	Date	Mileage	Comments
Essential Checks			
Air Filters			
Batteries			
Battery / Alternator			
Belts & Hoses			
Brakes Serviced			
Chassis			
Fan Belts			
Fluid Levels			
Fuel Filter			
Heater & Radiator Hose			
Lights			
Oil Change			
Radiator			
Rotate / Balance Tires			
Spark Plugs			
Transmission			
Water Pump			
Wheel Alignment			
Wipers			
Secondary Checks			
Dump Value			
Fire Extinguisher			
Furnace			
Generator			
Material Seams			
Refrigerator			
Satellite / Antenna			
Steps			
Stove			
Water			
Water Heater			
Water Tanks			
Window Seals			

	Date	Mileage	Comments
Inside			
Basin & Seals			
Carpet			
CO2 & Smoke Alarms			
Countertops			
Door Latches			
Doors			
Fans / Air Con			
Fridge / Freezer			
Oven			
Power Points			
Shower Fixtures			
Sink & Seals			
Sky Lights			
Stove			
Toilet			
Upholstery			

Notes:

RV Maintenance Log Book

Date	Repairs / Maintenance	Comments

	Date	Mileage	Comments
Essential Checks			
Air Filters			
Batteries			
Battery / Alternator			
Belts & Hoses			
Brakes Serviced			
Chassis			
Fan Belts			
Fluid Levels			
Fuel Filter			
Heater & Radiator Hose			
Lights			
Oil Change			
Radiator			
Rotate / Balance Tires			
Spark Plugs			
Transmission			
Water Pump			
Wheel Alignment			
Wipers			
Secondary Checks			
Dump Value			
Fire Extinguisher			
Furnace			
Generator			
Material Seams			
Refrigerator			
Satellite / Antenna			
Steps			
Stove			
Water			
Water Heater			
Water Tanks			
Window Seals			

	Date	Mileage	Comments
Inside			
Basin & Seals			
Carpet			
CO2 & Smoke Alarms			
Countertops			
Door Latches			
Doors			
Fans / Air Con			
Fridge / Freezer			
Oven			
Power Points			
Shower Fixtures			
Sink & Seals			
Sky Lights			
Stove			
Toilet			
Upholstery			

Notes:

RV Maintenance Log Book

Date	Repairs / Maintenance	Comments

	Date	Mileage	Comments
Essential Checks			
Air Filters			
Batteries			
Battery / Alternator			
Belts & Hoses			
Brakes Serviced			
Chassis			
Fan Belts			
Fluid Levels			
Fuel Filter			
Heater & Radiator Hose			
Lights			
Oil Change			
Radiator			
Rotate / Balance Tires			
Spark Plugs			
Transmission			
Water Pump			
Wheel Alignment			
Wipers			
Secondary Checks			
Dump Value			
Fire Extinguisher			
Furnace			
Generator			
Material Seams			
Refrigerator			
Satellite / Antenna			
Steps			
Stove			
Water			
Water Heater			
Water Tanks			
Window Seals			

	Date	Mileage	Comments
Inside			
Basin & Seals			
Carpet			
CO2 & Smoke Alarms			
Countertops			
Door Latches			
Doors			
Fans / Air Con			
Fridge / Freezer			
Oven			
Power Points			
Shower Fixtures			
Sink & Seals			
Sky Lights			
Stove			
Toilet			
Upholstery			

Notes:

RV Maintenance Log Book

Date	Repairs / Maintenance	Comments

	Date	Mileage	Comments
Essential Checks			
Air Filters			
Batteries			
Battery / Alternator			
Belts & Hoses			
Brakes Serviced			
Chassis			
Fan Belts			
Fluid Levels			
Fuel Filter			
Heater & Radiator Hose			
Lights			
Oil Change			
Radiator			
Rotate / Balance Tires			
Spark Plugs			
Transmission			
Water Pump			
Wheel Alignment			
Wipers			
Secondary Checks			
Dump Value			
Fire Extinguisher			
Furnace			
Generator			
Material Seams			
Refrigerator			
Satellite / Antenna			
Steps			
Stove			
Water			
Water Heater			
Water Tanks			
Window Seals			

	Date	Mileage	Comments
Inside			
Basin & Seals			
Carpet			
CO2 & Smoke Alarms			
Countertops			
Door Latches			
Doors			
Fans / Air Con			
Fridge / Freezer			
Oven			
Power Points			
Shower Fixtures			
Sink & Seals			
Sky Lights			
Stove			
Toilet			
Upholstery			

Notes:

RV Maintenance Log Book

Date	Repairs / Maintenance	Comments

	Date	Mileage	Comments
Essential Checks			
Air Filters			
Batteries			
Battery / Alternator			
Belts & Hoses			
Brakes Serviced			
Chassis			
Fan Belts			
Fluid Levels			
Fuel Filter			
Heater & Radiator Hose			
Lights			
Oil Change			
Radiator			
Rotate / Balance Tires			
Spark Plugs			
Transmission			
Water Pump			
Wheel Alignment			
Wipers			
Secondary Checks			
Dump Value			
Fire Extinguisher			
Furnace			
Generator			
Material Seams			
Refrigerator			
Satellite / Antenna			
Steps			
Stove			
Water			
Water Heater			
Water Tanks			
Window Seals			

	Date	Mileage	Comments
Inside			
Basin & Seals			
Carpet			
CO2 & Smoke Alarms			
Countertops			
Door Latches			
Doors			
Fans / Air Con			
Fridge / Freezer			
Oven			
Power Points			
Shower Fixtures			
Sink & Seals			
Sky Lights			
Stove			
Toilet			
Upholstery			

Notes:

RV Maintenance Log Book

Date	Repairs / Maintenance	Comments

	Date	Mileage	Comments
Essential Checks			
Air Filters			
Batteries			
Battery / Alternator			
Belts & Hoses			
Brakes Serviced			
Chassis			
Fan Belts			
Fluid Levels			
Fuel Filter			
Heater & Radiator Hose			
Lights			
Oil Change			
Radiator			
Rotate / Balance Tires			
Spark Plugs			
Transmission			
Water Pump			
Wheel Alignment			
Wipers			
Secondary Checks			
Dump Value			
Fire Extinguisher			
Furnace			
Generator			
Material Seams			
Refrigerator			
Satellite / Antenna			
Steps			
Stove			
Water			
Water Heater			
Water Tanks			
Window Seals			

	Date	Mileage	Comments
Inside			
Basin & Seals			
Carpet			
CO2 & Smoke Alarms			
Countertops			
Door Latches			
Doors			
Fans / Air Con			
Fridge / Freezer			
Oven			
Power Points			
Shower Fixtures			
Sink & Seals			
Sky Lights			
Stove			
Toilet			
Upholstery			

Notes:

RV Maintenance Log Book

Date	Repairs / Maintenance	Comments

	Date	Mileage	Comments
Essential Checks			
Air Filters			
Batteries			
Battery / Alternator			
Belts & Hoses			
Brakes Serviced			
Chassis			
Fan Belts			
Fluid Levels			
Fuel Filter			
Heater & Radiator Hose			
Lights			
Oil Change			
Radiator			
Rotate / Balance Tires			
Spark Plugs			
Transmission			
Water Pump			
Wheel Alignment			
Wipers			
Secondary Checks			
Dump Value			
Fire Extinguisher			
Furnace			
Generator			
Material Seams			
Refrigerator			
Satellite / Antenna			
Steps			
Stove			
Water			
Water Heater			
Water Tanks			
Window Seals			

	Date	Mileage	Comments
Inside			
Basin & Seals			
Carpet			
CO2 & Smoke Alarms			
Countertops			
Door Latches			
Doors			
Fans / Air Con			
Fridge / Freezer			
Oven			
Power Points			
Shower Fixtures			
Sink & Seals			
Sky Lights			
Stove			
Toilet			
Upholstery			

Notes:

RV Maintenance Log Book

Date	Repairs / Maintenance	Comments

	Date	Mileage	Comments
Essential Checks			
Air Filters			
Batteries			
Battery / Alternator			
Belts & Hoses			
Brakes Serviced			
Chassis			
Fan Belts			
Fluid Levels			
Fuel Filter			
Heater & Radiator Hose			
Lights			
Oil Change			
Radiator			
Rotate / Balance Tires			
Spark Plugs			
Transmission			
Water Pump			
Wheel Alignment			
Wipers			
Secondary Checks			
Dump Value			
Fire Extinguisher			
Furnace			
Generator			
Material Seams			
Refrigerator			
Satellite / Antenna			
Steps			
Stove			
Water			
Water Heater			
Water Tanks			
Window Seals			

	Date	Mileage	Comments
Inside			
Basin & Seals			
Carpet			
CO2 & Smoke Alarms			
Countertops			
Door Latches			
Doors			
Fans / Air Con			
Fridge / Freezer			
Oven			
Power Points			
Shower Fixtures			
Sink & Seals			
Sky Lights			
Stove			
Toilet			
Upholstery			

Notes:

RV Maintenance Log Book

Date	Repairs / Maintenance	Comments

	Date	Mileage	Comments
Essential Checks			
Air Filters			
Batteries			
Battery / Alternator			
Belts & Hoses			
Brakes Serviced			
Chassis			
Fan Belts			
Fluid Levels			
Fuel Filter			
Heater & Radiator Hose			
Lights			
Oil Change			
Radiator			
Rotate / Balance Tires			
Spark Plugs			
Transmission			
Water Pump			
Wheel Alignment			
Wipers			
Secondary Checks			
Dump Value			
Fire Extinguisher			
Furnace			
Generator			
Material Seams			
Refrigerator			
Satellite / Antenna			
Steps			
Stove			
Water			
Water Heater			
Water Tanks			
Window Seals			

	Date	Mileage	Comments
Inside			
Basin & Seals			
Carpet			
CO2 & Smoke Alarms			
Countertops			
Door Latches			
Doors			
Fans / Air Con			
Fridge / Freezer			
Oven			
Power Points			
Shower Fixtures			
Sink & Seals			
Sky Lights			
Stove			
Toilet			
Upholstery			

Notes:

RV Maintenance Log Book

Date	Repairs / Maintenance	Comments

	Date	Mileage	Comments
Essential Checks			
Air Filters			
Batteries			
Battery / Alternator			
Belts & Hoses			
Brakes Serviced			
Chassis			
Fan Belts			
Fluid Levels			
Fuel Filter			
Heater & Radiator Hose			
Lights			
Oil Change			
Radiator			
Rotate / Balance Tires			
Spark Plugs			
Transmission			
Water Pump			
Wheel Alignment			
Wipers			
Secondary Checks			
Dump Value			
Fire Extinguisher			
Furnace			
Generator			
Material Seams			
Refrigerator			
Satellite / Antenna			
Steps			
Stove			
Water			
Water Heater			
Water Tanks			
Window Seals			

	Date	Mileage	Comments
Inside			
Basin & Seals			
Carpet			
CO2 & Smoke Alarms			
Countertops			
Door Latches			
Doors			
Fans / Air Con			
Fridge / Freezer			
Oven			
Power Points			
Shower Fixtures			
Sink & Seals			
Sky Lights			
Stove			
Toilet			
Upholstery			

Notes:

RV Maintenance Log Book

Date	Repairs / Maintenance	Comments

	Date	Mileage	Comments
Essential Checks			
Air Filters			
Batteries			
Battery / Alternator			
Belts & Hoses			
Brakes Serviced			
Chassis			
Fan Belts			
Fluid Levels			
Fuel Filter			
Heater & Radiator Hose			
Lights			
Oil Change			
Radiator			
Rotate / Balance Tires			
Spark Plugs			
Transmission			
Water Pump			
Wheel Alignment			
Wipers			
Secondary Checks			
Dump Value			
Fire Extinguisher			
Furnace			
Generator			
Material Seams			
Refrigerator			
Satellite / Antenna			
Steps			
Stove			
Water			
Water Heater			
Water Tanks			
Window Seals			

	Date	Mileage	Comments
Inside			
Basin & Seals			
Carpet			
CO2 & Smoke Alarms			
Countertops			
Door Latches			
Doors			
Fans / Air Con			
Fridge / Freezer			
Oven			
Power Points			
Shower Fixtures			
Sink & Seals			
Sky Lights			
Stove			
Toilet			
Upholstery			

Notes:

RV Maintenance Log Book

Date	Repairs / Maintenance	Comments

	Date	Mileage	Comments
Essential Checks			
Air Filters			
Batteries			
Battery / Alternator			
Belts & Hoses			
Brakes Serviced			
Chassis			
Fan Belts			
Fluid Levels			
Fuel Filter			
Heater & Radiator Hose			
Lights			
Oil Change			
Radiator			
Rotate / Balance Tires			
Spark Plugs			
Transmission			
Water Pump			
Wheel Alignment			
Wipers			
Secondary Checks			
Dump Value			
Fire Extinguisher			
Furnace			
Generator			
Material Seams			
Refrigerator			
Satellite / Antenna			
Steps			
Stove			
Water			
Water Heater			
Water Tanks			
Window Seals			

	Date	Mileage	Comments
Inside			
Basin & Seals			
Carpet			
CO2 & Smoke Alarms			
Countertops			
Door Latches			
Doors			
Fans / Air Con			
Fridge / Freezer			
Oven			
Power Points			
Shower Fixtures			
Sink & Seals			
Sky Lights			
Stove			
Toilet			
Upholstery			

Notes:

RV Maintenance Log Book

Date	Repairs / Maintenance	Comments

	Date	Mileage	Comments
Essential Checks			
Air Filters			
Batteries			
Battery / Alternator			
Belts & Hoses			
Brakes Serviced			
Chassis			
Fan Belts			
Fluid Levels			
Fuel Filter			
Heater & Radiator Hose			
Lights			
Oil Change			
Radiator			
Rotate / Balance Tires			
Spark Plugs			
Transmission			
Water Pump			
Wheel Alignment			
Wipers			
Secondary Checks			
Dump Value			
Fire Extinguisher			
Furnace			
Generator			
Material Seams			
Refrigerator			
Satellite / Antenna			
Steps			
Stove			
Water			
Water Heater			
Water Tanks			
Window Seals			

	Date	Mileage	Comments
Inside			
Basin & Seals			
Carpet			
CO2 & Smoke Alarms			
Countertops			
Door Latches			
Doors			
Fans / Air Con			
Fridge / Freezer			
Oven			
Power Points			
Shower Fixtures			
Sink & Seals			
Sky Lights			
Stove			
Toilet			
Upholstery			

Notes:

RV Maintenance Log Book

Date	Repairs / Maintenance	Comments

	Date	Mileage	Comments
Essential Checks			
Air Filters			
Batteries			
Battery / Alternator			
Belts & Hoses			
Brakes Serviced			
Chassis			
Fan Belts			
Fluid Levels			
Fuel Filter			
Heater & Radiator Hose			
Lights			
Oil Change			
Radiator			
Rotate / Balance Tires			
Spark Plugs			
Transmission			
Water Pump			
Wheel Alignment			
Wipers			
Secondary Checks			
Dump Value			
Fire Extinguisher			
Furnace			
Generator			
Material Seams			
Refrigerator			
Satellite / Antenna			
Steps			
Stove			
Water			
Water Heater			
Water Tanks			
Window Seals			

	Date	Mileage	Comments
Inside			
Basin & Seals			
Carpet			
CO2 & Smoke Alarms			
Countertops			
Door Latches			
Doors			
Fans / Air Con			
Fridge / Freezer			
Oven			
Power Points			
Shower Fixtures			
Sink & Seals			
Sky Lights			
Stove			
Toilet			
Upholstery			

Notes:

RV Maintenance Log Book

Date	Repairs / Maintenance	Comments

	Date	Mileage	Comments
Essential Checks			
Air Filters			
Batteries			
Battery / Alternator			
Belts & Hoses			
Brakes Serviced			
Chassis			
Fan Belts			
Fluid Levels			
Fuel Filter			
Heater & Radiator Hose			
Lights			
Oil Change			
Radiator			
Rotate / Balance Tires			
Spark Plugs			
Transmission			
Water Pump			
Wheel Alignment			
Wipers			
Secondary Checks			
Dump Value			
Fire Extinguisher			
Furnace			
Generator			
Material Seams			
Refrigerator			
Satellite / Antenna			
Steps			
Stove			
Water			
Water Heater			
Water Tanks			
Window Seals			

	Date	Mileage	Comments
Inside			
Basin & Seals			
Carpet			
CO2 & Smoke Alarms			
Countertops			
Door Latches			
Doors			
Fans / Air Con			
Fridge / Freezer			
Oven			
Power Points			
Shower Fixtures			
Sink & Seals			
Sky Lights			
Stove			
Toilet			
Upholstery			

Notes:

RV Maintenance Log Book

Date	Repairs / Maintenance	Comments

	Date	Mileage	Comments
Essential Checks			
Air Filters			
Batteries			
Battery / Alternator			
Belts & Hoses			
Brakes Serviced			
Chassis			
Fan Belts			
Fluid Levels			
Fuel Filter			
Heater & Radiator Hose			
Lights			
Oil Change			
Radiator			
Rotate / Balance Tires			
Spark Plugs			
Transmission			
Water Pump			
Wheel Alignment			
Wipers			
Secondary Checks			
Dump Value			
Fire Extinguisher			
Furnace			
Generator			
Material Seams			
Refrigerator			
Satellite / Antenna			
Steps			
Stove			
Water			
Water Heater			
Water Tanks			
Window Seals			

	Date	Mileage	Comments
Inside			
Basin & Seals			
Carpet			
CO2 & Smoke Alarms			
Countertops			
Door Latches			
Doors			
Fans / Air Con			
Fridge / Freezer			
Oven			
Power Points			
Shower Fixtures			
Sink & Seals			
Sky Lights			
Stove			
Toilet			
Upholstery			

Notes:

RV Maintenance Log Book

Date	Repairs / Maintenance	Comments

	Date	Mileage	Comments
Essential Checks			
Air Filters			
Batteries			
Battery / Alternator			
Belts & Hoses			
Brakes Serviced			
Chassis			
Fan Belts			
Fluid Levels			
Fuel Filter			
Heater & Radiator Hose			
Lights			
Oil Change			
Radiator			
Rotate / Balance Tires			
Spark Plugs			
Transmission			
Water Pump			
Wheel Alignment			
Wipers			
Secondary Checks			
Dump Value			
Fire Extinguisher			
Furnace			
Generator			
Material Seams			
Refrigerator			
Satellite / Antenna			
Steps			
Stove			
Water			
Water Heater			
Water Tanks			
Window Seals			

	Date	Mileage	Comments
Inside			
Basin & Seals			
Carpet			
CO2 & Smoke Alarms			
Countertops			
Door Latches			
Doors			
Fans / Air Con			
Fridge / Freezer			
Oven			
Power Points			
Shower Fixtures			
Sink & Seals			
Sky Lights			
Stove			
Toilet			
Upholstery			

Notes:

RV Maintenance Log Book

Date	Repairs / Maintenance	Comments

	Date	Mileage	Comments
Essential Checks			
Air Filters			
Batteries			
Battery / Alternator			
Belts & Hoses			
Brakes Serviced			
Chassis			
Fan Belts			
Fluid Levels			
Fuel Filter			
Heater & Radiator Hose			
Lights			
Oil Change			
Radiator			
Rotate / Balance Tires			
Spark Plugs			
Transmission			
Water Pump			
Wheel Alignment			
Wipers			
Secondary Checks			
Dump Value			
Fire Extinguisher			
Furnace			
Generator			
Material Seams			
Refrigerator			
Satellite / Antenna			
Steps			
Stove			
Water			
Water Heater			
Water Tanks			
Window Seals			

	Date	Mileage	Comments
Inside			
Basin & Seals			
Carpet			
CO2 & Smoke Alarms			
Countertops			
Door Latches			
Doors			
Fans / Air Con			
Fridge / Freezer			
Oven			
Power Points			
Shower Fixtures			
Sink & Seals			
Sky Lights			
Stove			
Toilet			
Upholstery			

Notes:

RV Maintenance Log Book

Date	Repairs / Maintenance	Comments

	Date	Mileage	Comments
Essential Checks			
Air Filters			
Batteries			
Battery / Alternator			
Belts & Hoses			
Brakes Serviced			
Chassis			
Fan Belts			
Fluid Levels			
Fuel Filter			
Heater & Radiator Hose			
Lights			
Oil Change			
Radiator			
Rotate / Balance Tires			
Spark Plugs			
Transmission			
Water Pump			
Wheel Alignment			
Wipers			
Secondary Checks			
Dump Value			
Fire Extinguisher			
Furnace			
Generator			
Material Seams			
Refrigerator			
Satellite / Antenna			
Steps			
Stove			
Water			
Water Heater			
Water Tanks			
Window Seals			

	Date	Mileage	Comments
Inside			
Basin & Seals			
Carpet			
CO2 & Smoke Alarms			
Countertops			
Door Latches			
Doors			
Fans / Air Con			
Fridge / Freezer			
Oven			
Power Points			
Shower Fixtures			
Sink & Seals			
Sky Lights			
Stove			
Toilet			
Upholstery			

Notes:

RV Maintenance Log Book

Date	Repairs / Maintenance	Comments

	Date	Mileage	Comments
Essential Checks			
Air Filters			
Batteries			
Battery / Alternator			
Belts & Hoses			
Brakes Serviced			
Chassis			
Fan Belts			
Fluid Levels			
Fuel Filter			
Heater & Radiator Hose			
Lights			
Oil Change			
Radiator			
Rotate / Balance Tires			
Spark Plugs			
Transmission			
Water Pump			
Wheel Alignment			
Wipers			
Secondary Checks			
Dump Value			
Fire Extinguisher			
Furnace			
Generator			
Material Seams			
Refrigerator			
Satellite / Antenna			
Steps			
Stove			
Water			
Water Heater			
Water Tanks			
Window Seals			

	Date	Mileage	Comments
Inside			
Basin & Seals			
Carpet			
CO2 & Smoke Alarms			
Countertops			
Door Latches			
Doors			
Fans / Air Con			
Fridge / Freezer			
Oven			
Power Points			
Shower Fixtures			
Sink & Seals			
Sky Lights			
Stove			
Toilet			
Upholstery			

Notes:

RV Maintenance Log Book

Date	Repairs / Maintenance	Comments

	Date	Mileage	Comments
Essential Checks			
Air Filters			
Batteries			
Battery / Alternator			
Belts & Hoses			
Brakes Serviced			
Chassis			
Fan Belts			
Fluid Levels			
Fuel Filter			
Heater & Radiator Hose			
Lights			
Oil Change			
Radiator			
Rotate / Balance Tires			
Spark Plugs			
Transmission			
Water Pump			
Wheel Alignment			
Wipers			
Secondary Checks			
Dump Value			
Fire Extinguisher			
Furnace			
Generator			
Material Seams			
Refrigerator			
Satellite / Antenna			
Steps			
Stove			
Water			
Water Heater			
Water Tanks			
Window Seals			

	Date	Mileage	Comments
Inside			
Basin & Seals			
Carpet			
CO2 & Smoke Alarms			
Countertops			
Door Latches			
Doors			
Fans / Air Con			
Fridge / Freezer			
Oven			
Power Points			
Shower Fixtures			
Sink & Seals			
Sky Lights			
Stove			
Toilet			
Upholstery			

Notes:

RV Maintenance Log Book

Date	Repairs / Maintenance	Comments

	Date	Mileage	Comments
Essential Checks			
Air Filters			
Batteries			
Battery / Alternator			
Belts & Hoses			
Brakes Serviced			
Chassis			
Fan Belts			
Fluid Levels			
Fuel Filter			
Heater & Radiator Hose			
Lights			
Oil Change			
Radiator			
Rotate / Balance Tires			
Spark Plugs			
Transmission			
Water Pump			
Wheel Alignment			
Wipers			
Secondary Checks			
Dump Value			
Fire Extinguisher			
Furnace			
Generator			
Material Seams			
Refrigerator			
Satellite / Antenna			
Steps			
Stove			
Water			
Water Heater			
Water Tanks			
Window Seals			

	Date	Mileage	Comments
Inside			
Basin & Seals			
Carpet			
CO2 & Smoke Alarms			
Countertops			
Door Latches			
Doors			
Fans / Air Con			
Fridge / Freezer			
Oven			
Power Points			
Shower Fixtures			
Sink & Seals			
Sky Lights			
Stove			
Toilet			
Upholstery			

Notes:

RV Maintenance Log Book

Date	Repairs / Maintenance	Comments

	Date	Mileage	Comments
Essential Checks			
Air Filters			
Batteries			
Battery / Alternator			
Belts & Hoses			
Brakes Serviced			
Chassis			
Fan Belts			
Fluid Levels			
Fuel Filter			
Heater & Radiator Hose			
Lights			
Oil Change			
Radiator			
Rotate / Balance Tires			
Spark Plugs			
Transmission			
Water Pump			
Wheel Alignment			
Wipers			
Secondary Checks			
Dump Value			
Fire Extinguisher			
Furnace			
Generator			
Material Seams			
Refrigerator			
Satellite / Antenna			
Steps			
Stove			
Water			
Water Heater			
Water Tanks			
Window Seals			

	Date	Mileage	Comments
Inside			
Basin & Seals			
Carpet			
CO2 & Smoke Alarms			
Countertops			
Door Latches			
Doors			
Fans / Air Con			
Fridge / Freezer			
Oven			
Power Points			
Shower Fixtures			
Sink & Seals			
Sky Lights			
Stove			
Toilet			
Upholstery			

Notes:

RV Maintenance Log Book

Date	Repairs / Maintenance	Comments

	Date	Mileage	Comments
Essential Checks			
Air Filters			
Batteries			
Battery / Alternator			
Belts & Hoses			
Brakes Serviced			
Chassis			
Fan Belts			
Fluid Levels			
Fuel Filter			
Heater & Radiator Hose			
Lights			
Oil Change			
Radiator			
Rotate / Balance Tires			
Spark Plugs			
Transmission			
Water Pump			
Wheel Alignment			
Wipers			
Secondary Checks			
Dump Value			
Fire Extinguisher			
Furnace			
Generator			
Material Seams			
Refrigerator			
Satellite / Antenna			
Steps			
Stove			
Water			
Water Heater			
Water Tanks			
Window Seals			

	Date	Mileage	Comments
Inside			
Basin & Seals			
Carpet			
CO2 & Smoke Alarms			
Countertops			
Door Latches			
Doors			
Fans / Air Con			
Fridge / Freezer			
Oven			
Power Points			
Shower Fixtures			
Sink & Seals			
Sky Lights			
Stove			
Toilet			
Upholstery			

Notes:

RV Maintenance Log Book

Date	Repairs / Maintenance	Comments

	Date	Mileage	Comments
Essential Checks			
Air Filters			
Batteries			
Battery / Alternator			
Belts & Hoses			
Brakes Serviced			
Chassis			
Fan Belts			
Fluid Levels			
Fuel Filter			
Heater & Radiator Hose			
Lights			
Oil Change			
Radiator			
Rotate / Balance Tires			
Spark Plugs			
Transmission			
Water Pump			
Wheel Alignment			
Wipers			
Secondary Checks			
Dump Value			
Fire Extinguisher			
Furnace			
Generator			
Material Seams			
Refrigerator			
Satellite / Antenna			
Steps			
Stove			
Water			
Water Heater			
Water Tanks			
Window Seals			

	Date	Mileage	Comments
Inside			
Basin & Seals			
Carpet			
CO2 & Smoke Alarms			
Countertops			
Door Latches			
Doors			
Fans / Air Con			
Fridge / Freezer			
Oven			
Power Points			
Shower Fixtures			
Sink & Seals			
Sky Lights			
Stove			
Toilet			
Upholstery			

Notes:

RV Maintenance Log Book

Date	Repairs / Maintenance	Comments

	Date	Mileage	Comments
Essential Checks			
Air Filters			
Batteries			
Battery / Alternator			
Belts & Hoses			
Brakes Serviced			
Chassis			
Fan Belts			
Fluid Levels			
Fuel Filter			
Heater & Radiator Hose			
Lights			
Oil Change			
Radiator			
Rotate / Balance Tires			
Spark Plugs			
Transmission			
Water Pump			
Wheel Alignment			
Wipers			
Secondary Checks			
Dump Value			
Fire Extinguisher			
Furnace			
Generator			
Material Seams			
Refrigerator			
Satellite / Antenna			
Steps			
Stove			
Water			
Water Heater			
Water Tanks			
Window Seals			

	Date	Mileage	Comments
Inside			
Basin & Seals			
Carpet			
CO2 & Smoke Alarms			
Countertops			
Door Latches			
Doors			
Fans / Air Con			
Fridge / Freezer			
Oven			
Power Points			
Shower Fixtures			
Sink & Seals			
Sky Lights			
Stove			
Toilet			
Upholstery			

Notes:

RV Maintenance Log Book

Date	Repairs / Maintenance	Comments

	Date	Mileage	Comments
Essential Checks			
Air Filters			
Batteries			
Battery / Alternator			
Belts & Hoses			
Brakes Serviced			
Chassis			
Fan Belts			
Fluid Levels			
Fuel Filter			
Heater & Radiator Hose			
Lights			
Oil Change			
Radiator			
Rotate / Balance Tires			
Spark Plugs			
Transmission			
Water Pump			
Wheel Alignment			
Wipers			
Secondary Checks			
Dump Value			
Fire Extinguisher			
Furnace			
Generator			
Material Seams			
Refrigerator			
Satellite / Antenna			
Steps			
Stove			
Water			
Water Heater			
Water Tanks			
Window Seals			

	Date	Mileage	Comments
Inside			
Basin & Seals			
Carpet			
CO2 & Smoke Alarms			
Countertops			
Door Latches			
Doors			
Fans / Air Con			
Fridge / Freezer			
Oven			
Power Points			
Shower Fixtures			
Sink & Seals			
Sky Lights			
Stove			
Toilet			
Upholstery			

Notes:

RV Maintenance Log Book

Date	Repairs / Maintenance	Comments

	Date	Mileage	Comments
Essential Checks			
Air Filters			
Batteries			
Battery / Alternator			
Belts & Hoses			
Brakes Serviced			
Chassis			
Fan Belts			
Fluid Levels			
Fuel Filter			
Heater & Radiator Hose			
Lights			
Oil Change			
Radiator			
Rotate / Balance Tires			
Spark Plugs			
Transmission			
Water Pump			
Wheel Alignment			
Wipers			
Secondary Checks			
Dump Value			
Fire Extinguisher			
Furnace			
Generator			
Material Seams			
Refrigerator			
Satellite / Antenna			
Steps			
Stove			
Water			
Water Heater			
Water Tanks			
Window Seals			

	Date	Mileage	Comments
Inside			
Basin & Seals			
Carpet			
CO2 & Smoke Alarms			
Countertops			
Door Latches			
Doors			
Fans / Air Con			
Fridge / Freezer			
Oven			
Power Points			
Shower Fixtures			
Sink & Seals			
Sky Lights			
Stove			
Toilet			
Upholstery			

Notes:

RV Maintenance Log Book

Date	Repairs / Maintenance	Comments

	Date	Mileage	Comments
Essential Checks			
Air Filters			
Batteries			
Battery / Alternator			
Belts & Hoses			
Brakes Serviced			
Chassis			
Fan Belts			
Fluid Levels			
Fuel Filter			
Heater & Radiator Hose			
Lights			
Oil Change			
Radiator			
Rotate / Balance Tires			
Spark Plugs			
Transmission			
Water Pump			
Wheel Alignment			
Wipers			
Secondary Checks			
Dump Value			
Fire Extinguisher			
Furnace			
Generator			
Material Seams			
Refrigerator			
Satellite / Antenna			
Steps			
Stove			
Water			
Water Heater			
Water Tanks			
Window Seals			

	Date	Mileage	Comments
Inside			
Basin & Seals			
Carpet			
CO2 & Smoke Alarms			
Countertops			
Door Latches			
Doors			
Fans / Air Con			
Fridge / Freezer			
Oven			
Power Points			
Shower Fixtures			
Sink & Seals			
Sky Lights			
Stove			
Toilet			
Upholstery			

Notes:

RV Maintenance Log Book

Date	Repairs / Maintenance	Comments

	Date	Mileage	Comments
Essential Checks			
Air Filters			
Batteries			
Battery / Alternator			
Belts & Hoses			
Brakes Serviced			
Chassis			
Fan Belts			
Fluid Levels			
Fuel Filter			
Heater & Radiator Hose			
Lights			
Oil Change			
Radiator			
Rotate / Balance Tires			
Spark Plugs			
Transmission			
Water Pump			
Wheel Alignment			
Wipers			
Secondary Checks			
Dump Value			
Fire Extinguisher			
Furnace			
Generator			
Material Seams			
Refrigerator			
Satellite / Antenna			
Steps			
Stove			
Water			
Water Heater			
Water Tanks			
Window Seals			

	Date	Mileage	Comments
Inside			
Basin & Seals			
Carpet			
CO2 & Smoke Alarms			
Countertops			
Door Latches			
Doors			
Fans / Air Con			
Fridge / Freezer			
Oven			
Power Points			
Shower Fixtures			
Sink & Seals			
Sky Lights			
Stove			
Toilet			
Upholstery			

Notes:

RV Maintenance Log Book

Date	Repairs / Maintenance	Comments

	Date	Mileage	Comments
Essential Checks			
Air Filters			
Batteries			
Battery / Alternator			
Belts & Hoses			
Brakes Serviced			
Chassis			
Fan Belts			
Fluid Levels			
Fuel Filter			
Heater & Radiator Hose			
Lights			
Oil Change			
Radiator			
Rotate / Balance Tires			
Spark Plugs			
Transmission			
Water Pump			
Wheel Alignment			
Wipers			
Secondary Checks			
Dump Value			
Fire Extinguisher			
Furnace			
Generator			
Material Seams			
Refrigerator			
Satellite / Antenna			
Steps			
Stove			
Water			
Water Heater			
Water Tanks			
Window Seals			

	Date	Mileage	Comments
Inside			
Basin & Seals			
Carpet			
CO2 & Smoke Alarms			
Countertops			
Door Latches			
Doors			
Fans / Air Con			
Fridge / Freezer			
Oven			
Power Points			
Shower Fixtures			
Sink & Seals			
Sky Lights			
Stove			
Toilet			
Upholstery			

Notes:

RV Maintenance Log Book

Date	Repairs / Maintenance	Comments

	Date	Mileage	Comments
Essential Checks			
Air Filters			
Batteries			
Battery / Alternator			
Belts & Hoses			
Brakes Serviced			
Chassis			
Fan Belts			
Fluid Levels			
Fuel Filter			
Heater & Radiator Hose			
Lights			
Oil Change			
Radiator			
Rotate / Balance Tires			
Spark Plugs			
Transmission			
Water Pump			
Wheel Alignment			
Wipers			
Secondary Checks			
Dump Value			
Fire Extinguisher			
Furnace			
Generator			
Material Seams			
Refrigerator			
Satellite / Antenna			
Steps			
Stove			
Water			
Water Heater			
Water Tanks			
Window Seals			

	Date	Mileage	Comments
Inside			
Basin & Seals			
Carpet			
CO2 & Smoke Alarms			
Countertops			
Door Latches			
Doors			
Fans / Air Con			
Fridge / Freezer			
Oven			
Power Points			
Shower Fixtures			
Sink & Seals			
Sky Lights			
Stove			
Toilet			
Upholstery			

Notes:

RV Maintenance Log Book

Date	Repairs / Maintenance	Comments

	Date	Mileage	Comments
Essential Checks			
Air Filters			
Batteries			
Battery / Alternator			
Belts & Hoses			
Brakes Serviced			
Chassis			
Fan Belts			
Fluid Levels			
Fuel Filter			
Heater & Radiator Hose			
Lights			
Oil Change			
Radiator			
Rotate / Balance Tires			
Spark Plugs			
Transmission			
Water Pump			
Wheel Alignment			
Wipers			
Secondary Checks			
Dump Value			
Fire Extinguisher			
Furnace			
Generator			
Material Seams			
Refrigerator			
Satellite / Antenna			
Steps			
Stove			
Water			
Water Heater			
Water Tanks			
Window Seals			

	Date	Mileage	Comments
Inside			
Basin & Seals			
Carpet			
CO2 & Smoke Alarms			
Countertops			
Door Latches			
Doors			
Fans / Air Con			
Fridge / Freezer			
Oven			
Power Points			
Shower Fixtures			
Sink & Seals			
Sky Lights			
Stove			
Toilet			
Upholstery			

Notes:

RV Maintenance Log Book

Date	Repairs / Maintenance	Comments

	Date	Mileage	Comments
Essential Checks			
Air Filters			
Batteries			
Battery / Alternator			
Belts & Hoses			
Brakes Serviced			
Chassis			
Fan Belts			
Fluid Levels			
Fuel Filter			
Heater & Radiator Hose			
Lights			
Oil Change			
Radiator			
Rotate / Balance Tires			
Spark Plugs			
Transmission			
Water Pump			
Wheel Alignment			
Wipers			
Secondary Checks			
Dump Value			
Fire Extinguisher			
Furnace			
Generator			
Material Seams			
Refrigerator			
Satellite / Antenna			
Steps			
Stove			
Water			
Water Heater			
Water Tanks			
Window Seals			

	Date	Mileage	Comments
Inside			
Basin & Seals			
Carpet			
CO2 & Smoke Alarms			
Countertops			
Door Latches			
Doors			
Fans / Air Con			
Fridge / Freezer			
Oven			
Power Points			
Shower Fixtures			
Sink & Seals			
Sky Lights			
Stove			
Toilet			
Upholstery			

Notes:

RV Maintenance Log Book

Date	Repairs / Maintenance	Comments

	Date	Mileage	Comments
Essential Checks			
Air Filters			
Batteries			
Battery / Alternator			
Belts & Hoses			
Brakes Serviced			
Chassis			
Fan Belts			
Fluid Levels			
Fuel Filter			
Heater & Radiator Hose			
Lights			
Oil Change			
Radiator			
Rotate / Balance Tires			
Spark Plugs			
Transmission			
Water Pump			
Wheel Alignment			
Wipers			
Secondary Checks			
Dump Value			
Fire Extinguisher			
Furnace			
Generator			
Material Seams			
Refrigerator			
Satellite / Antenna			
Steps			
Stove			
Water			
Water Heater			
Water Tanks			
Window Seals			

	Date	Mileage	Comments
Inside			
Basin & Seals			
Carpet			
CO2 & Smoke Alarms			
Countertops			
Door Latches			
Doors			
Fans / Air Con			
Fridge / Freezer			
Oven			
Power Points			
Shower Fixtures			
Sink & Seals			
Sky Lights			
Stove			
Toilet			
Upholstery			

Notes:

RV Maintenance Log Book

Date	Repairs / Maintenance	Comments

	Date	Mileage	Comments
Essential Checks			
Air Filters			
Batteries			
Battery / Alternator			
Belts & Hoses			
Brakes Serviced			
Chassis			
Fan Belts			
Fluid Levels			
Fuel Filter			
Heater & Radiator Hose			
Lights			
Oil Change			
Radiator			
Rotate / Balance Tires			
Spark Plugs			
Transmission			
Water Pump			
Wheel Alignment			
Wipers			
Secondary Checks			
Dump Value			
Fire Extinguisher			
Furnace			
Generator			
Material Seams			
Refrigerator			
Satellite / Antenna			
Steps			
Stove			
Water			
Water Heater			
Water Tanks			
Window Seals			

	Date	Mileage	Comments
Inside			
Basin & Seals			
Carpet			
CO2 & Smoke Alarms			
Countertops			
Door Latches			
Doors			
Fans / Air Con			
Fridge / Freezer			
Oven			
Power Points			
Shower Fixtures			
Sink & Seals			
Sky Lights			
Stove			
Toilet			
Upholstery			

Notes:

RV Maintenance Log Book

Date	Repairs / Maintenance	Comments

	Date	Mileage	Comments
Essential Checks			
Air Filters			
Batteries			
Battery / Alternator			
Belts & Hoses			
Brakes Serviced			
Chassis			
Fan Belts			
Fluid Levels			
Fuel Filter			
Heater & Radiator Hose			
Lights			
Oil Change			
Radiator			
Rotate / Balance Tires			
Spark Plugs			
Transmission			
Water Pump			
Wheel Alignment			
Wipers			
Secondary Checks			
Dump Value			
Fire Extinguisher			
Furnace			
Generator			
Material Seams			
Refrigerator			
Satellite / Antenna			
Steps			
Stove			
Water			
Water Heater			
Water Tanks			
Window Seals			

	Date	Mileage	Comments
Inside			
Basin & Seals			
Carpet			
CO2 & Smoke Alarms			
Countertops			
Door Latches			
Doors			
Fans / Air Con			
Fridge / Freezer			
Oven			
Power Points			
Shower Fixtures			
Sink & Seals			
Sky Lights			
Stove			
Toilet			
Upholstery			

Notes:

RV Maintenance Log Book

Date	Repairs / Maintenance	Comments

	Date	Mileage	Comments
Essential Checks			
Air Filters			
Batteries			
Battery / Alternator			
Belts & Hoses			
Brakes Serviced			
Chassis			
Fan Belts			
Fluid Levels			
Fuel Filter			
Heater & Radiator Hose			
Lights			
Oil Change			
Radiator			
Rotate / Balance Tires			
Spark Plugs			
Transmission			
Water Pump			
Wheel Alignment			
Wipers			
Secondary Checks			
Dump Value			
Fire Extinguisher			
Furnace			
Generator			
Material Seams			
Refrigerator			
Satellite / Antenna			
Steps			
Stove			
Water			
Water Heater			
Water Tanks			
Window Seals			

	Date	Mileage	Comments
Inside			
Basin & Seals			
Carpet			
CO2 & Smoke Alarms			
Countertops			
Door Latches			
Doors			
Fans / Air Con			
Fridge / Freezer			
Oven			
Power Points			
Shower Fixtures			
Sink & Seals			
Sky Lights			
Stove			
Toilet			
Upholstery			

Notes:

RV Maintenance Log Book

Date	Repairs / Maintenance	Comments

	Date	Mileage	Comments
Essential Checks			
Air Filters			
Batteries			
Battery / Alternator			
Belts & Hoses			
Brakes Serviced			
Chassis			
Fan Belts			
Fluid Levels			
Fuel Filter			
Heater & Radiator Hose			
Lights			
Oil Change			
Radiator			
Rotate / Balance Tires			
Spark Plugs			
Transmission			
Water Pump			
Wheel Alignment			
Wipers			
Secondary Checks			
Dump Value			
Fire Extinguisher			
Furnace			
Generator			
Material Seams			
Refrigerator			
Satellite / Antenna			
Steps			
Stove			
Water			
Water Heater			
Water Tanks			
Window Seals			

	Date	Mileage	Comments
Inside			
Basin & Seals			
Carpet			
CO2 & Smoke Alarms			
Countertops			
Door Latches			
Doors			
Fans / Air Con			
Fridge / Freezer			
Oven			
Power Points			
Shower Fixtures			
Sink & Seals			
Sky Lights			
Stove			
Toilet			
Upholstery			

Notes:

RV Maintenance Log Book

Date	Repairs / Maintenance	Comments

	Date	Mileage	Comments
Essential Checks			
Air Filters			
Batteries			
Battery / Alternator			
Belts & Hoses			
Brakes Serviced			
Chassis			
Fan Belts			
Fluid Levels			
Fuel Filter			
Heater & Radiator Hose			
Lights			
Oil Change			
Radiator			
Rotate / Balance Tires			
Spark Plugs			
Transmission			
Water Pump			
Wheel Alignment			
Wipers			
Secondary Checks			
Dump Value			
Fire Extinguisher			
Furnace			
Generator			
Material Seams			
Refrigerator			
Satellite / Antenna			
Steps			
Stove			
Water			
Water Heater			
Water Tanks			
Window Seals			

	Date	Mileage	Comments
Inside			
Basin & Seals			
Carpet			
CO2 & Smoke Alarms			
Countertops			
Door Latches			
Doors			
Fans / Air Con			
Fridge / Freezer			
Oven			
Power Points			
Shower Fixtures			
Sink & Seals			
Sky Lights			
Stove			
Toilet			
Upholstery			

Notes:

RV Maintenance Log Book

Date	Repairs / Maintenance	Comments

	Date	Mileage	Comments
Essential Checks			
Air Filters			
Batteries			
Battery / Alternator			
Belts & Hoses			
Brakes Serviced			
Chassis			
Fan Belts			
Fluid Levels			
Fuel Filter			
Heater & Radiator Hose			
Lights			
Oil Change			
Radiator			
Rotate / Balance Tires			
Spark Plugs			
Transmission			
Water Pump			
Wheel Alignment			
Wipers			
Secondary Checks			
Dump Value			
Fire Extinguisher			
Furnace			
Generator			
Material Seams			
Refrigerator			
Satellite / Antenna			
Steps			
Stove			
Water			
Water Heater			
Water Tanks			
Window Seals			

	Date	Mileage	Comments
Inside			
Basin & Seals			
Carpet			
CO2 & Smoke Alarms			
Countertops			
Door Latches			
Doors			
Fans / Air Con			
Fridge / Freezer			
Oven			
Power Points			
Shower Fixtures			
Sink & Seals			
Sky Lights			
Stove			
Toilet			
Upholstery			

Notes:

RV Maintenance Log Book

Date	Repairs / Maintenance	Comments

Thank you—Please Help...

Thank you so much for purchasing this RV Repair And Maintenance Log Book. I truly hope you find it useful and you have every success using it.

I would be delighted if you could please spare 2 minutes and leave a brief review of this journal on Amazon. It helps me enormously.

Simply visit Amazon and type in the name of this book.

"RV Repair And Maintenance Log Book — Peter Log"

Please find the book and click the link. Then scroll down to where you will see the reviews (there might not be any if it's a new book). Click the 'Write Customer Review' button and leave your review.

Write a customer review

That's it—it will take about 2 minutes and I will massively appreciate it. It will help such a lot. Thank you again,

Best wishes
Peter Log

Made in the USA
San Bernardino, CA
05 July 2020